# THE GROTTO WAS MY HEAVEN

Fr John Lochran

# 'The Grotto was my Heaven'
## — *St Bernadette*

## MEDITATIONS ON
## THE MESSAGE OF LOURDES

THE COLUMBA PRESS
DUBLIN 1993

First edition, 1993, published by
THE COLUMBA PRESS
93 The Rise, Mount Merrion, Blackrock, Co Dublin, Ireland

Cover and illustrations by Bill Bolger
origination by The Columba Press
Printed by Loader Jackson Printers, Arlesey

ISBN 1 85607 075 1

The author and publisher gratefully acknowledge the
permission of Sanctuaire de Notre-Dame, Lourdes, to
reproduce the photographs of Bernadette and the assistance
of Photo Lacaze, Lourdes, who supplied the prints.

# Contents

# Contents

# Preface

Father John Lochran is a Scottish priest and former missionary in Africa.

In 1985, he was appointed Chaplain to the English-speaking pilgrims to Lourdes. Having lived and prayed in the Shrine of Our Lady of Lourdes, he has discovered the presence of Mary in his own life and through his apostolate amongst the pilgrims. He is a privileged witness to the wonders God accomplishes daily in the lives of the millions who come here.

At Lourdes, through the words and gestures of Bernadette, God invites us to follow more deeply the way of the gospel. Mary leads us as she did Bernadette, to a deeper knowledge of her Son, Jesus Christ. Bernadette 'met' Mary and through that meeting Bernadette was able to read her life more clearly in the light of the gospels. Her poverty becomes that of Jesus who is born among the poor and lowly. Her prayer reveals the experience of the 'other world'. Her compassion for sinners testifies to the passion of Christ and her service to the Church reminds us of our call to be co-workers in the mission of Christ.

In the spirit of his missionary vocation, Father John wished to share with us some of his reflections on this deep, rich and meaningful message that is Lourdes. In pondering his written testimony I invite you, the reader, to the spring made known to Bernadette by Mary, and which is the merciful heart of Jesus.

Our grateful thanks to Father John Lochran. May these words enable each of you to walk with Bernadette along the pilgrim's road towards the intimate love of the Father.

*Father Joseph Bordes*
*Rector of the Shrine of*
*Our Lady of Lourdes*

# Introduction

In 1985 I was appointed Chaplain in Lourdes for the English-speaking pilgrims. To serve as a chaplain of Our Lady of Lourdes is always an honour for any priest. To me it meant so much more. It was a gracious gift of a merciful and loving God who, in bringing me to Lourdes, gave me new life, new hope and a new mission.

The story of my coming to Lourdes really began in a place thousands of miles away from Europe and the Pyrenean mountains; indeed, in a most unlikely spot within the heart of an altogether different continent, Africa. As a young missionary priest I had been sent to Zaire, the former Belgian Congo. There, as I now realize, the mysterious ways of Divine Providence moved to guide my steps on the path of a personal pilgrimage to Lourdes and a rendezvous with God's healing love.

At the entrance to the mission where I worked in Zaire was a huge statue of Our Lady of Lourdes. I began to notice a poor African stumble his way to that statue day after day. He could barely walk or speak, his arms were completely paralyzed and his eyes were fixed in some strange trance. I discovered he had been poisoned by some members of his tribe in an act of revenge. My heart was filled with pity as I saw him, day after day, limp along the road towards Mary. Little did I know then that, within a short period of time, I too would be limping along the road towards Mary, coming before her, broken in body and spirit, to kneel at her feet at the Grotto of Lourdes.

In Zaire I became very ill. It was a sudden and serious illness that worsened each day and spanned a period of two years. Along with physical suffering came a nightmare of pain and frustration, a time of vacillation between hope and almost utter despair. I felt abandoned by the Lord. The future, if there was to be any, looked bleak. It was in this moment of impasse that the Lord in his mercy touched my life. Led by his hand I found myself in Lourdes before the heart of Mary. Not only was I healed, but through a whole series of events I came to be Chaplain for the English-speaking pilgrims. Such are the wonderful ways of God's mercy.

To be physically well and active again was certainly a great favour. But there was another healing that took place, of a more important kind – that of the heart. It was a healing of all the bitterness and resentment, pride and anguish, fear and desolation that had grown within me. It was, above all, these sicknesses that the Lord wished to heal and, in doing so, to enable me to become an instrument of his healing love and reconciliation for many who would come to this Marian Shrine.

The reflections I would like to share with you have been written for all those who, like me and my poor African brother, 'limp along the road towards God', especially those who are handicapped by the burdens of the heart and long to know the tender mercy of God. It was Bernadette who said, 'The Grotto was my heaven.'

I hope you will find in these reflections something of that 'heaven', something of that deeply personal love that Bernadette experienced and which God wishes to bestow upon us all. I hope they will be a help to you in a pilgrimage to Lourdes and for that longer pilgrimage you make daily towards the heart of the living God.

*Father John Lochran*
*Chaplain of Lourdes*

# 'GOOD FOR NOTHING'

*'Give me the bread of humility.*
*Give me the bread of charity,*
*the bread of seeing you alone in all things*
*and at all times'*

Not everyone, like Our Lady, smiled upon Bernadette. Indeed, Sister Marie Terese Vauzou, Bernadette's novice mistress and future Superior General of the order, was heard to say, 'If Our Lady wanted to appear on earth why did she choose to do so to such an ignorant, uneducated little peasant when she could have chosen a holy and well-educated nun?' However wrong the sister was in her assessment of the ways of God, Bernadette would not have disagreed with the nun's assessment of her. In fact she went far beyond the Sister's opinion by describing herself as a 'good for nothing'. It was in fact a committed belief, a lived experience. She had no great ability or aptitude for anything, neither for the things of heaven nor the things of earth. She couldn't grasp the difficult formulas of the catechism or lessons at school. She remained an ignorant, illiterate peasant. Sickness added to that experience of her own uselessness. And so she was as she said, and experience proclaimed, a 'good for nothing'.

But to the nun's question, St Paul replied that God 'chose those who count for nothing to reduce to nothing all those who do count for something' (1 Cor 1:28-29). Bernadette was a witness to God's choice and preference of the poor, the lowly, the humble of heart. Bernadette was poor in what we consider to be important, but rich in the truly important. She was destitute, uneducated and sick. But she had a heart that understood the essential. She was a 'good for nothing' but a 'good for nothing' loved by God. And *this* is the essential!

At Lourdes, God chose someone who, in the eyes of the world, had no value, one of the forgotten of the earth. The advent of a Presence, the arrival of Mary, turns upside down the criteria we often nurture in our assessment of life, and shatters the illusions we so often create about our world. Lourdes is in fact the rehabilitation by God of the poor, the humiliated, the oppressed. It is the presence of hope at the centre of what seems to be the most useless – sickness, suffering, poverty.

Perhaps what we fear most in life is this – to be considered as good for nothing, useless, inefficient, ignored, rejected, without value. Here lies the importance of Lourdes for it raises the question 'What value has our life?' We do not come to Lourdes just for words or ceremonies or processions. In the light of the apparitions and the Gospels, we come to relearn from God himself the value of our lives.

Bernadette becomes a symbol of the poor and lowly of the earth. She reminds us that our value does not come from what we have or how we are, but rather depends upon the free gift of love of Another; that God's love is before all else; that God is not drawn to us by our great intellects, our abilities, our achievements, our success, but by our littleness, our humility. In contrast to the beatitudes of the world stand the beatitudes of the Gospel. Not happy are those who boast in themselves for having 'it made' in this world, but 'happy the poor in spirit...'; those who 'boast in the Lord' for having 'been made' in the image of his love and open to the treasures of the kingdom of heaven. It is the happiness of the poor and the humble who, with Mary in the *Magnificat*, can sing the joy of their hearts in praising the Lord for looking upon them in their 'nothingness' and loving them.

The poor are not those who have nothing. They are those who know they have received everything. Indeed I cannot think of anything that God has neglected for us. Everything has been given. We have a God who leaves all the glory of heaven to dwell among us, who comes himself in littleness and poverty to share our condition and draw near us. A God who on the cross says 'This is how much you are loved by me'. A God who has given us all the sacraments to take care of our every need from birth to death.

Bernadette saw that such a God could only be *love* and nothing else. That love, by nature, could not remain alone, but had to give itself, to share, to restore, to reconcile, to make one. It is the God of Jesus Christ who, looking upon our nothingness, desires to 'make the deaf hear and the dumb speak, the blind to see, the lame to walk and to raise the dead to life' (Mt 11:4-6).

The sick, and all those who come to Lourdes, broken in body and in spirit, are brothers together on the Way of the Cross. But they tell us of a solidarity greater than that of being sick and oppressed. Like Bernadette, they witness to another solidarity, the solidarity of those whom God has chosen; the weak and the lowly. They witness the oneness of God with the lost, the hopeless, and the crucified of the earth. 'I was hungry and you gave me to eat, sick and you came to visit...'(Mt 25).

'Good for nothing?' Experience may say so, but God never will. 'I have loved you with an everlasting love'(Jer 31:3). 'Your name is written on the palm of my hand' (Is 49:16). This is the value he places on us. Not because of any merit on our part. Not because of our intelligence or status or wealth or ability. But just because – just because to God it is so!

'OH MARY, MY DEAR MOTHER,
I CAN'T TAKE ANY MORE...'

*'I am happier on my sick bed with my
crucifix, than a queen upon her throne'*

Over the years I have come to realize that many pilgrims who come to Lourdes don't really grasp the full significance of Bernadette's life and especially her suffering. Yes, we know that somehow she suffered, but the fact of Mary's appearing to her seems in some way to render it more 'acceptable'. Certainly, if we focus our attention merely on the apparitions we can easily make the mistake of seeing the whole story as some kind of fairy tale, like Cinderella being visited by the fairy God-mother. The story of Bernadette is no fairy tale. It involves real people whose real lives are shaped, not by the wave of a magic wand, but rather by a much deeper vision of love. Instead of centring our attention on the apparitions we have to consider the whole context of Bernadette's life. If we are to grasp her importance for us today, if we are to understand the deeper message of Lourdes and allow this to have an impact on how we think, act and live, then we cannot afford to ignore the great suffering she had to contend with.

In 1858 life for the Soubirous was far from easy. A family of six lived in one room, the Cachot, an old prison unfit for human habitation. They had no money, no bread, and almost no hope. Death and disease were never far from their door. So hungry were they that Bernadette's little brother was found eating candle wax in the parish Church during the time of the apparitions. Sharing her family misery, Bernadette had her own sorrows to live. At school she had to suffer all kinds of humiliation as the dunce of the 'paupers' class'. She was always sick, a situation that the apparitions did not change. In fact the apparitions brought an even greater martyrdom. They caused mockery, incomprehension, threats, interrogations and opposition. She had to make the sacrifice of leaving Lourdes and her family for exile in the convent of Nevers.

In the face of trials and suffering we either run or rebel. We become bitter and resentful, venting our anger upon God for all the misfortune that comes our way. We even fear that suffering is a punishment for our sins. I have been guilty of such reactions myself. I'm sure God understands our weakness, our fear, and perhaps our cowardice. Even the holy men of the Bible cried out in anger against God in the midst of their agony.

But this is not Bernadette's way. No complaining, no anger, no bitterness, no rebellion against God. 'If God allows it then you shouldn't complain.' An expression of a fatalistic resignation to pain? Not at all. It wasn't that God wanted her to suffer. People in Lourdes could have come to her aid and that of the family. This is what God would have wanted. Just as God wants everyone, in a spirit of fraternity, to take up their responsibilities in order to resolve much of the suffering present in our world today. It wasn't that Bernadette enjoyed suffering. She certainly didn't and stated so quite clearly. 'Oh Mary, my dear mother, I can't take any more…,' doesn't imply a glorious carrying of the Cross. But she followed the Way of the Cross right to the end as Mary herself had done. She neither runs nor rebels because she is humbly open to Another who in his own death and resurrection has promised that life, not death, has the last word. This is where Bernadette finds her hope and her courage. She believes firmly and deeply in a God who loves her, who truly desires her happiness. What sustained Bernadette in the midst of her trials is found at the heart of the Bible, the promise of God. A promise not for our destruction, but for our welfare, not for death but for resurrection.

I have heard priests, preaching at Lourdes, telling the sick how noble it is to suffer. I cannot understand or accept this. Have they never suffered themselves? How can you tell a mother whose child is horribly mangled and chained to a wheelchair that suffering is noble? Suffering is not noble, it is ugly. Didn't Jesus himself, faced with the passion, not have a 'sorrow unto death?' Jesus didn't come to glorify suffering. He came to glorify his Father's love. If he allows himself to suffer, it is not to tell us how wonderful suffering is, but how wonderful God's love is. If he allows himself to die on the cross, it is for no masochistic intent, but rather to show us to what extent we are precious in his eyes. Jesus didn't come to teach us how to die but how to live. He calls us, not to some fatalistic acceptance of our pain, but to face that pain with him and to allow him to transform our darkness into light through the power of the resurrection.

Bernadette kept on going through her Way of the Cross, not because of any strength or ability of her own, but rather because of her reliance on Another who never regrets his own creation, on one who pledges himself in our favour in every page of the Gospels. She keeps on going because in her humility she is open to all the promises of Christ. 'Come to me you who are burdened; learn from me for I am gentle and humble of heart; do not let your hearts be troubled; hope in God, trust in him still; I have come for the lost sheep; I am the resurrection and the life; whoever believes in me will never die.'

Our bitterness, resentment, and rebellion are the opposite of the man of the Gospels, of the man of the beatitudes. 'How happy are the poor in spirit for theirs is the kingdom of heaven; how happy are those who suffer for they shall be comforted.' When Jesus said these words he didn't intend to glorify suffering. He does not say how happy are those who are poor because they are poor, but rather because to them belongs the kingdom of heaven. He does not say happy those who suffer because they hurt, but because they will be comforted. Our bitterness and resentment prevents us from being open to these promises of God and can enslave us to a form of pride that closes our hearts to a God who is the source and guarantee of what is best for us.

When God frees the Israelites from Egypt he does not lead them immediately into the promised land. Instead, he takes them into the desert. He doesn't spare them from the difficulties of life. But not in order to crush them. Rather he wants them to go farther on their journey, to go to a deeper freedom and a greater understanding and trust in his love. Sometimes we are allowed to feel that 'desert' experience ourselves – those failings, perplexities and trials that come to us all as we journey through life. With God we needn't give up or run away; with him they can be confronted and overcome in a way that allows us to enter the deeper reality of the 'promised land' of his love.

Jesus never said life would be easy. He never made such a promise. What he did promise was 'In the world you will have trouble, but be brave for I have conquered the world' (Jn 16:33). Bernadette is a beacon for us of that victory over the trials and tribulations of life. She points the way for each of us towards a more humble and loving confidence in the One who is the giver of life.

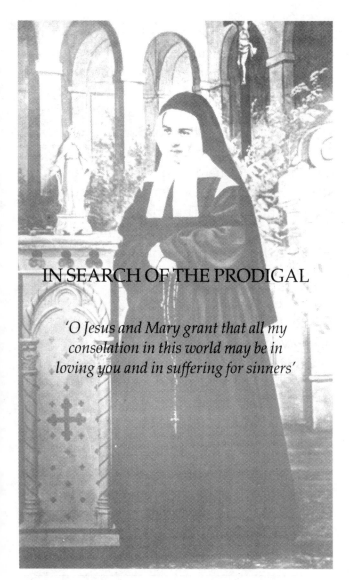

# IN SEARCH OF THE PRODIGAL

*'O Jesus and Mary grant that all my
consolation in this world may be in
loving you and in suffering for sinners'*

A winter's night at the Grotto. My eyes wandered from the statue of Our Lady to the cold, hard, frozen ground below. 'Would you be so kind as to kiss the ground for sinners?', I remembered Mary saying to Bernadette. What sinners? I wondered. Those of Bernadette's time? Certainly. But then Mary wasn't bound by space and time as we are. The thought suddenly struck me that maybe Bernadette had kissed the ground for me. That maybe she had made this sacrificial act of love for all the people, all sinners who come in pilgrimage to Lourdes. It was a humbling thought.

'Kiss the ground for sinners.' Wasn't it exactly this that Jesus had done in leaving all the glory of heaven, in being born in a stable at Bethlehem, to embrace the 'ground' that is humanity? Didn't he come to bring a kiss of life to the sick, the lost, the sinful – to announce to all humanity, 'Your sins have been forgiven you'?

'Holy Mary, Mother of God, pray for us sinners.' We describe ourselves as 'sinners', not children, or friends, or servants, or faithful, but sinners. And we *are* sinners. We have no difficulty in admitting it. Even those of no religious persuasion do so. Just look at the people so ready to 'confess' their sins on television, radio, in magazines and newspapers. Great is the human need to tell its sin. The telling of it seems to provide a kind of liberation, an assurance of paying our debt, of expiating and exorcising our woes, as if the admission alone can bridge the gap between right and wrong, between sinner and God. But this is *not* the nature of reconciliation announced by the gospel. It is not that of being paid for, or expiated by us. Rather it is a gift freely given by God in Jesus Christ who bestows upon us a pardon we have no right to merit.

'Kiss the ground for sinners.' An act freely and lovingly performed by Bernadette. A gift of pardon and mercy freely given by Jesus on the cross. The embrace of heaven and earth for all time as Jesus pronounces the bountiful words of the most radical love ever, 'Father, forgive them for they know not what they do.' (Lk 23:24).

'Know not what they do'? Yes, we know that we are sinners, but not in the way we think. Real sin is of a deeper nature than a simple admission of weakness. The joy of the confessor is that of heaven 'over one sinner who repents'. His sadness is to see hearts who 'know not what they do', who do not see the sin behind the 'sins', our refusal to admit our radical incapacity to love. Confession bothers us. We are skillful in justifying ourselves, in making excuses; slow to recognize the truth. Like the pharisee in the Temple, we are quick to assert that we are not 'like other men' (Lk 18:12), but deaf to the publican crying out 'God be merciful to me a sinner' (Lk 18.14). It is only the real prodigal who can say, 'Father, I have sinned against heaven and against you' (Lk 15:18).

The place chosen by Our Lady to appear to Bernadette, the place known as Massabielle, was a rocky recess where the river washed up all kinds of driftwood, refuse, rubbish and debris. It was also a pig-sty. It was a reminder of the refuse and rubbish that surface on the shores of humanity; of the violence, hatred, injustice and oppression of our world; of the selfishness that dwells in our heart. But it is also a reminder of the forgiveness and mercy God holds out to us. The pig-sty evokes the prodigal, the lost son who, having squandered everything, ends up with the pigs. In the Gospel story we are told that 'he came to his senses', he recognized his utter misery and saw he was better off in his Father's house. It is only when we come to our senses that true conversion begins to take place. Only when we are fundamentally convinced that we cannot grow without the love of a caring Father can we begin our return towards him.

And yet even our admission of sin can become itself an obstacle on the road of our return. Sometimes we are like Adam in the Garden. Having sinned and seen his nakedness, Adam runs to hide from God. When we are confronted with our sins and failures we fear an angry God in search of reprisal. We stop at our sin, we fear God, we do not wish to appear naked before him, found with our ugliness. We are blocked by a despairing kind of pride that believes God could never love such sinful people. Stopping at our sin we lose all sight of God's compassion and fail to grasp the very heart of the Good News, that we are already forgiven on the cross; that God loves us not because we are good but because he is good; that Jesus comes not for the righteous but for sinners, not to condemn but to enter into the very wounds of our hearts to heal and bring new life.

Beneath the mud of the pig-sty Mary led Bernadette to discover a spring of water. Beyond the mud that symbolizes our sin flows another water, that which symbolizes Jesus' love for us poured out upon the cross. This is the water we can 'go drink and wash in', the water that cleanses, refreshes, gives life. The Lord never resents the gift of life he has given us. In seeing the prodigal a 'long way off', he rushes to meet him, not to condemn or rebuke, not to treat him as his sin would merit, but rather to give him the best; not condemnation, but celebration, for the 'one who was dead has come to life, he who was lost is found' (Lk 15:30-31).

The real miracle that Lourdes proposes to us, more than that of the body, is that of the heart, that of our conversion. But it is the only miracle that God cannot accomplish without our participation. Man's recognition of his own radical weakness is the only way he will come to feel his utter need of God's help.

Mary calls us not to be afraid of the sin that fills our heart; to turn back to God not in spite of our weakness but because of it. The message of Lourdes calls us not to be afraid of the anguish and guilt we have in not loving enough, but rather to place it where it belongs, before the heart and within the hands of Christ.

What was once a rubbish dump, once a pig-sty, is now a place of God's presence, a place of prayer, caring and brotherhood. This is what God wishes to do with our hearts; to transform us, to heal us of our darkness, to recreate us in his image. Mary points us to the heart of the gospel, God in search of the prodigal to bring him back home.

# 'THE GROTTO WAS MY HEAVEN'

*'I carry the Grotto in my heart'*

'Mary set out at that time and went as quickly as she could into the hill country…'(Lk 1:39). Such are the opening words of the story of the Visitation. Within this gospel story of a simple act of charity of one cousin for another, lies the very essence of the mystery of God's love for humankind and the mystery of our own lives. Mary and Elizabeth meet together in a joy that is immense, a joy that expresses the wonderful design that God has upon them and through them for all humankind.

For years Elizabeth had suffered the humiliation of being sterile. Now the humiliation is over. Touched by the Holy Spirit she is made fertile; she is to bear a child. Mary, as a pious Jewish girl, carried in her heart all the humiliations of her own people, all the poverty, misery and oppression of the Jewish nation. And she held too in her heart the hope of a Saviour, a Messiah who would come to save his people. Now, that Saviour was present in her very womb. The message of the Visitation is really the first fruits of the Incarnation itself. God has not abandoned his people to evil and misery but has come to embrace humankind within his own heart.

In 1858, Mary set out again to visit another 'hill country', this time that of the Pyrenean mountains. She set out to tell Bernadette and the whole world this same Gospel message. The image of Mary appearing to Bernadette in what was then a pig-sty reflects the very fabric of the Incarnation of Jesus leaving all the glory of heaven to enter into the poverty, misery and sinfulness of humankind.

At that time in her own life, Bernadette, like Mary and Elizabeth before her, had known such great humiliation. Indeed it was a moment of radical impasse in her life. As she set out to gather firewood on that day of the 11th of February 1858, who knows what burdens must have weighed in her heart. But in setting out to collect firewood, little did Bernadette realize that another fuel was waiting to warm her heart, that of love. Like Pentecost, it all began with sound like a rush of wind, symbol of the Holy Spirit coming to herald the arrival of Mary and to breathe new hope into the heart of this humble child.

'Virgin of Light, you are the smile of a God who loves us'. So begins an evening hymn to Mary frequently sung in Lourdes. To Bernadette she smiles. To Bernadette she reveals the image of the true God. Not that of a remote, impersonal power, not that of an angry, tyrannical being who plays capricious games with his people, but that of the God who 'hears the cry of his people in distress' (Ex 3:7-8); who delivers them for the joys of the promised land.

In naming herself to Bernadette as the 'Immaculate Conception', Mary does more than remind us of her great privilege as 'woman blessed among all women' (Lk 1:12). It is also the affirmation that the 'purest of creatures', in visiting the pig-sty of Lourdes, has not abandoned her children. Within the confines of time and history, within the world of a child's heart, Mary comes to lead us back to the mystery of the Incarnation, to the gospels, to the good news that 'God is with us' (Mt 1:18-23).

Mary thus reveals to Bernadette more than a smile. She reveals the burning love of God for humankind. The good news that Jesus announced is that the God who gave us life has a name. He is 'Father'. He is 'love'. In his preaching, Jesus reveals the 'Father' of the parables who searches for man more than man searches for him. He reveals him even more in his gestures of pardon, reconciliation and resurrection. Here is a God totally unexpected and unimaginable. Not the God of the doctors of the law, the scribes and the pharisees, who expected a God made in the same image as their own extreme, severe, judgmental ways. No, this is the 'Father' of the prodigal (Lk 15:28), the God of Jesus Christ, who goes out into the 'highways and byways' to invite us to the feast of his kingdom. A God not calling us to be 'appeased' but appearing as a beggar of our love.

It is the 'smile of God' that made Bernadette exclaim 'The Grotto was my Heaven'. For there, in the visit of Mary, all the richness of God's love and yearning for our hearts is made known; to feel loved and to love. Here is Bernadette's heaven, the heaven Mary invites us all to possess.

IN A CAVE BY A RIVER ...
ON THE ROADS WHERE WE WALK

*'Cross of Jesus You are the tree of life,
the mysterious ladder joining heaven
and earth.'*

41

Some years ago I said Mass in Lourdes for a group of young people from Kenya in Africa. Having myself been a missionary there, I thought I would use something from their own culture as a way of explaining the message of Lourdes. And so I spoke to them about certain caves found in Zanzibar, caves used during the time of the slave trade as holding pens for those awaiting deportation. Speaking to them about the physical slavery these caves evoked, I explained how Mary had appeared in a cave, the Grotto, to tell us of an even greater slavery, that of sin, and of the Lord's desire to bring us freedom.

At the end of the Mass came the amazing surprise. Just before leaving Africa to come to Lourdes, these young people had made a visit to these very caves in Zanzibar. They had no difficulty in grasping the message of my words. Some may say coincidence. I would say, clearly the hand of God; an amazing example of Divine Providence. In his own mysterious way God had prepared these young people for the message he had prepared me to give.

And yet we think that God does not speak to us in the concrete circumstances of our lives!

We have neither 'ears to hear nor eyes to see' as Jesus said (Mt 13). Rooted in blindness and indifference, slavishly held by the world around us, we fail to see the hand of God in our midst. That is one of the reasons why the apparitions of Our Lady to Bernadette are so important, for they tell us that God is not confined to heaven or the Temple. He is not held within the walls of our churches, but is there out on the roads we walk.

When Our Lady appeared to Bernadette it was not in a church, in what we might consider to be a recognized 'holy place'. Instead she appeared in a cave by a river. It is God's way of telling us that all life is holy for he is present in every detail. In the Bible examples abound. Abraham, a wandering nomad, gathers stones and builds altars at every stage of his travels (Gen 12); his way of saying that the whole world is God's cathedral. The story of Elijah is an even greater reminder of God's involvement in the affairs of men, and one of striking similarity with the story of the apparitions. Here again is the cave that for the holy men of the Bible is the place of refuge from storms and tempests, and above all the place of divine initiative. Elijah, in the midst of a terrible trial, in solitude and distress, takes refuge in a cave on Mt Horeb, the mountain of God. There he is visited by God, who makes his presence known by a light breeze. In the story of the apparitions, the visit of Mary is heralded by a sound like a rush of wind that awakens Bernadette's attention. Apart from Elijah, other prophets like Amos and Jeremiah, Isaiah and Daniel, are further witness to God's intervention in the very places and circumstances where their lives unfold. And then there is Moses. Upon approaching the burning bush, the voice of the Lord calls to him saying, 'Moses, the ground on which you stand is holy' (Ex 3:5-6). The Bible clearly tells us that the ground on which we stand, that is, all the circumstances of our lives, are holy because God is present in every detail of our world.

It is not Bernadette who goes in search of Mary, but the Blessed Virgin who looks for Bernadette. She knows to find her collecting firewood near the cave of Massabielle . Here is the image of God searching for his people that we find in the gospels. Jesus, who meets the disciples, not in the recognized 'holy places' of his time such as the Temple or synagogue, but rather in the places where they work, while they are fishing, collecting taxes and so on. He meets them on the roads where they live. And like Mary seeking Bernadette, he is first on the road. The God of Jesus Christ is not some remote impersonal God but one at the very heart of all we do and live. He is the God who 'eats and drinks with sinners' (Lk 7:31-35), supplies the wine for the wedding feast (Jn 2), and weeps over the death of his friend Lazarus (Jn 11).

Christianity is not intended as some kind of abstract knowledge 'about' God and unrelated to life. It is rather a living with God, a walking with him, a talking with him, a sharing with him, in our actual circumstances. Lourdes is a call for us to rediscover that indeed 'the Word was made flesh and dwells among us'. We are invited to meet him on the roads where we walk, in the places where we live. We are invited to find him already there searching for us, hoping to share with us the kingdom of his heart.

The presence of Jesus is not confined to the Temple or church. It is not limited to the Grotto or to Lourdes. Lourdes simply reminds us that all the 'ground on which we stand is holy'.

In a cave by a river Mary waited for Bernadette. On the roads where we walk Jesus waits
for us.

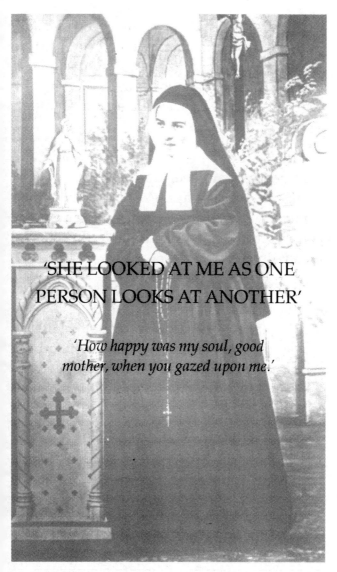

# 'SHE LOOKED AT ME AS ONE PERSON LOOKS AT ANOTHER'

*'How happy was my soul, good mother, when you gazed upon me.'*

There are looks that wound, despise, kill. Those that frown and bring fear. Those that are full of pride and condescension, that scorn and mock. Those that are full of anger and hatred. Worse still, there is no look at all – just indifference.

But there are other looks, that inspire hope and confidence, that cheer up and give new life. Looks of love that appreciate, value; that tell someone, whoever they may be, regardless of colour, creed, age, wealth or poverty: You, you mean something to me.

'She looked at me as one person looks at another.' Words of wonder, words of joy that well up from the heart of Bernadette. Perhaps it was the first time in her life she had been really noticed. Maybe the first time treated as a 'person', given such respect, tenderness, attention.

The eyes of Mary behold her in love; a look of love that gives life, invades a child's heart, inspires a courage that helps her in face of every opposition, gives her a confidence that compels the priests to build the church, to mould the shrine where pilgrims come today.

A look of love, a look of life.

Only the 'eyes of faith' can help us see the precious gift of life, the precious gift of love.

Only the 'eyes of the heart', enlightened by the Spirit, can open us to welcome and embrace each other as People of God, as one family of the same Father.

Today you have come as a pilgrim to Lourdes.
You have left your home, your family, your
       friends,
to find yourself among unknown faces.
A little lost in the crowd...
Searching for a look, a word,
a smile, not to feel alone.

Other pilgrims like you have also come,
to entrust their cares to Mary,
to pray, to beseech, to behold...
Each one with his own story, his own secret.

God also has a story for you, a secret to share.
He spoke it through the Prophets, reveals it in
       Jesus:

'Do not be afraid for I have redeemed you;
I have called you by your name, you are mine.
You are precious in my eyes and I love you.

Do not be afraid I am with you' (Is 32:1-5).

'As Jesus set out on a journey,
A man ran up and knelt before him;
Jesus looked steadily at him and loved him'
          (Mk 10:17,20).

So take heart and listen.
As God looked at Mary, as Mary looked at
          Bernadette,
So God looks at you with love.

As you pass along the streets of Lourdes,
look at the crowds going to the Grotto.
Sick, handicapped and healthy walk together
to approach the Blessed Virgin Mary.

Look at the man in the wheelchair,
the other who helps with his load.
See the face of your neighbour in prayer,
the hands that finger the Rosary beads...

See how the goodness of God
is written in the eyes of a child,
in the smile of a passer-by,
in the hands held out to help and care.
See the Crucified Jesus
in the crosses of those around you.

Look upon your fellow pilgrims

not as strangers, but as brothers
on the same road.
Look upon the sick and the handicapped
not as objects to be feared, but as persons
to embrace.

Today you are invited
to meet the liberating look of Jesus.
Let yourself be touched by his love.
Think of Jesus looking at Peter...
at the Samaritan woman...
at the one taken in adultery...
Think of how he looked on the sick
and the lost.
He forgave all, he healed many.

Do not be afraid.
Recognize your sin and your weakness.
Let yourself be renewed by the God who
loves you,
and with a new spirit, walk again
on the pilgrimage towards his heart.
As you find yourself in a sea of faces,
in a mass of humanity from every corner of
the earth,
do not think you have been forgotten,
for Mary looks at you 'as one person looks at
another'.

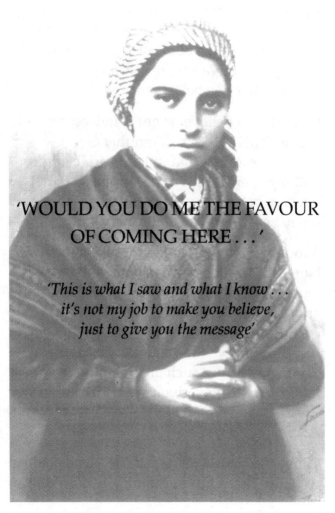

'WOULD YOU DO ME THE FAVOUR
OF COMING HERE . . . '

*'This is what I saw and what I know . . .
it's not my job to make you believe,
just to give you the message'*

In an interview for American television, when asked what I would say to sceptics, to those who have doubts about the story and message of Lourdes, my reply was that given by Bernadette to the people of her own time: 'My job is just to give you the message. It's up to you whether you believe it or not.'

Whether we believe or not is indeed for us to decide. This is the freedom that God gives us and he respects that freedom. He imposes nothing. Perhaps our real problem is not so much in believing or not, this or that message, but in hearing the message in the first place.

'Would you do me the favour of coming here?' Not command but invitation, not order but request, not imposition but entreaty … an invitation to leave everything else aside and come spend time with Mary. Bernadette was free to accept or reject the request. Of course, who could ever refuse such an invitation from Our Lady? Would we, given such a request, ever dream of refusing it? Of course we wouldn't. And yet we do, and often.

The appeal made to Bernadette is one made to us daily. Time and time again the Lord calls to each of us: 'Would you do me the favour of coming here?' 'Would you leave everything else aside and just be with me?' It is the invitation to prayer. A constant invitation. In all kinds of ways, both subtle and blunt, we manage to ignore it or not to hear the request at all. For we are busy people. Too busy with ourselves to think of the 'Father's affairs' (Lk2:49). Too busy being the Lord ourselves to allow someone else to be the centre of attention. Too busy dreaming of life elsewhere to live it differently now. Too busy with the pleasures and profits of the world to discover the 'pearl of great price in our midst' (Mt 13:45).

Lourdes appeals once more. In the image of Mary and Bernadette together at the Grotto we see the 'stuff' that prayer is made of. Not the 'babbling of pagans using many words to make themselves heard' that Jesus condemned, but an encounter between two hearts. A real prayer that goes beyond the mere recitation of words to become a union of two people held in an embrace of love. This is the prayer we are called to live. Not prayer for the saints alone, but for everyone. Not blind submission to a remote, omnipotent power or a vain search for an unknown God. What is offered is the humble quest of a God who, in the person of Jesus, comes to reveal his love and beg our love in return.

Before the unknown we are afraid. Before an unknown 'young lady', Bernadette was afraid. Her fear made her reach for her rosary beads. As she made the sign of the cross she began to feel at ease. The sign of the cross – invocation of Father, Son and Holy Spirit. The Trinity; a community of love. A community of love in whom there is no fear. A community of love in whom all our fears disappear. Prayer, like baptism, marked with the sign of the cross, is being plunged into this community of love where, surrounded by love, we feel at home. Prayer is not so much what we have to give to God, but is more a living with God, a 'meeting of one friend with another', a personal relationship in which it is truly God who does the giving, the giving of himself to us poor sinners.

'How happy I was, Oh good mother, to have the grace to gaze upon you'. True prayer is this constant looking upon, this being with, this faithful contemplation of the beauty and goodness of God that Bernadette experienced.

And one that will bring us happiness. Not the false illusions of happiness offered by this world, but the true happiness of the 'other world' promised to Bernadette. And this not as compensation in the hereafter for a painful earthly life, but the joy of a love that transforms everything here and now, and makes happiness possible whatever the circumstances. It was a sick person in Lourdes who said 'Hell is not to suffer, it is to suffer without love'.

To find ourselves with God in a heart-to-heart encounter; to love and allow ourselves to be loved. This is the secret of every Christian open to the good news of Jesus Christ. The secret of all who say yes to the gentle appeal, 'Would you do me the favour of coming here?'

# 'JUST A BROOM IN THE HANDS OF THE VIRGIN MARY'

*'I came here to hide myself'*

The feast of St Bernadette is held every year in Lourdes on the 18th of February. A special day; one that evokes a special memory of the first time I celebrated the feast as chaplain. On that particular occasion I had gone to say Mass for a group of people at the Cachot. Afterwards I went down to the Grotto to pray, and to venerate a relic of St Bernadette which is placed on the altar at the Grotto every year on her feast day. One of the workers employed by the shrine to keep the place tidy was there, busy sweeping away leaves from around the altar. He was using one of those old-fashioned brooms, the kind we think of in stories of witches. Anyway, at a certain moment he left the broom against the altar and went off to busy himself with other things. When he did this, when he left the broom against the altar, I really had to smile. I had to smile at the ways of God's providence. For, you see, someone once asked Bernadette if she was a saint and she replied 'No. I'm not a saint. I'm just a broom in the hands of the Virgin Mary.'

'Just a broom in the hands of the Virgin Mary.' Bernadette's description of herself. A simple instrument used by God, used by God to achieve so many great things. Like Mary she is a 'handmaid of the Lord'. All that God asked of her she did, not just at the time of the apparitions, but throughout her entire life. Bernadette wasn't canonized a saint because she saw Our Lady. She was canonized a saint because she *was* a saint, because in everything she tried to do the will of God, to fulfill the plan of life God had given her, to do all he had entrusted to her. And never more so than as a nun at the Convent of Nevers.

Indeed it was at the Convent of Nevers that Bernadette made her significant remark that gave to the broom such a providential and extraordinary meaning. Lourdes had only been the beginning. It is in Nevers, where Bernadette lived until her death at the age of 38, that her life as a humble religious sister proclaims what it really means to be a servant of the Lord. What to the world was an apparently useless, hidden existence was for Bernadette an experience of the deeper riches of life lived in union with Jesus. As we ponder this union of hearts that was lived out faithfully, lovingly, and ever more deeply, within the obscurity of the convent walls, we come to see more clearly than anywhere else all the innocence and docility, tenderness and humility, of a true child of God. It is this 'little broom' who reveals to us like no other saint the hidden wisdom of the Most High.

Here is the service of the humble and lowly of heart who are supple in God's hands, docile and open to the inspirations of his love. Here is the service of the real poor; not those who have nothing, but those who know they have received everything, that all is a gift from the hands of God. It is the service of those who recognize the presence of Another who is first in their lives, the source of all they have, the promise of all that will be. Bernadette was open to receive all from God, to learn his ways, and to allow him to shape the course of her life.

With St Paul she can say 'I have carried out the mission the Lord gave me' (Rom 15-19). With Jesus she can proclaim 'I have glorified you on earth and finished the work you gave me to do' (Jn 17:4).

Here is the poor humble servant of the Lord who questions and disturbs, provokes and prods consciences blind and indifferent to the ways of God and the deeper meaning of life. Her life demands and urges a radical revision of our quests for power and glory, self-interest and status, applause and adoration. Her docility in the service of God is a constant reminder not to put the Lord at our service but to be at his.

'Just a broom in the hands of the Virgin Mary.' Humility and service. The humble heart open to the ways of God, the willing heart ready to do the Lord's bidding. The Lord has a wonderful plan for our lives, just as he did for Bernadette. He calls each of us to play a part in the mission of his love for humankind. Holiness is not just for priests and nuns. Bernadette was a simple lay person chosen by God to be a witness and prophet of his love in the midst of the world.

'Just a broom in the hands of the Virgin Mary.' And what an effective broom she was. What happens in Lourdes today, a hundred and more years after the apparitions, bears witness to the effect of her instrumentality in the hands of God. A call to Bernadette, a call to each one of us to be a 'broom' in the hands of God, to be open to his designs on our hearts and lives, to be a humble servant in his work of reconciling the world to himself.

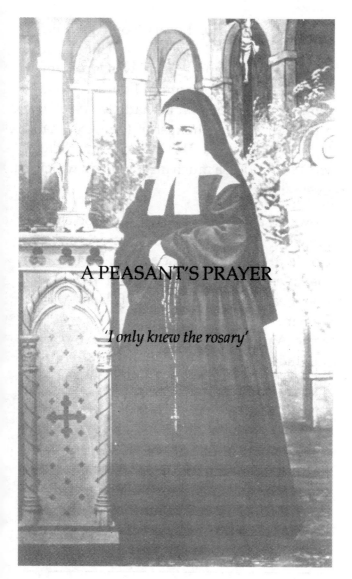

# A PEASANT'S PRAYER

*'I only knew the rosary'*

'I didn't know the Rosary could be such a beautiful prayer. I always thought it was a prayer for peasants.' Such was a comment made to me by a pilgrim in Lourdes. I had to remind the person that Bernadette herself was a peasant. That if the rest of the world had a heart half as good as this little peasant then the world would be a much nicer place in which to live!

How true and wonderful it is that God chooses the weak and the lowly to 'shame the wise' (1 Cor 1:25). Bernadette, the stupid, the ignorant, the illiterate. The one who cannot 'put into her poor head' all the complex doctrines of the catechism. The one who can neither read nor write. And yet here is the one chosen by God to tell the wise and learned of this world of another school where the deeper mysteries of life are to be learned, that of the rosary. This is her peasant's prayer, the school of her heart.

'I bless you Father, Lord of heaven and earth, for hiding these things from the learned and the clever and revealing them to mere children' (Mt 11:25-27). To a mere child the rosary became a school revealing all the wonders of God's love. The rosary taught Bernadette everything. To read the mystery of God's love for her. To write her response to that love in all the ordinary everyday events of her life. The rosary was her dictionary, her spelling book, naming and explaining the mysteries of God's kingdom; it was a map guiding her to the heart of God's love for mankind.

The 'Our Father' revealed the Father of all, his coming kingdom, the 'daily bread of his providence, the forgiveness of our sins.'

The 'Hail Mary' revealed a mother, blessed among women, giving Jesus to the world, embracing her and all poor sinners.

The 'Glory Be' – a hymn of praise to Father, Son and Holy Spirit … the Trinity; a community of love from whom all life comes, in whom life is, to whom life will always be.

The Fifteen Mysteries – it is these above all that opened to Bernadette all the magnitude of the merciful love of Jesus for humankind. Fifteen decades, fifteen stages of a journey through life. They are a path of life that Jesus follows from the Annunciation of his birth to his return to heaven. A pilgrimage of faith that Jesus makes in intimacy with the Father, a journey through the desert of the sinful world of humankind towards the promised land of his Father's love. It is the way for everyone, the journey, the pilgrimage that we all have to make toward the heart of the living God.

On every step of the journey Jesus makes, Mary is there with him. She is there in the joy of his birth, in Bethlehem, and in his life at Nazareth; in the sorrow of his sufferings and death on the cross. She shares in the glory of his resurrection. It is a journey through life she desires to make also with us. To be a companion through the joyful and sorrowful moments of our lives and to lead us to the glorious sharing in the mystery of God's love for us. This is her only concern. To see us taste, in and through Jesus, the intimate love of a Father's heart.

If we really pray the rosary – not saying it in some mechanical, routine way – if we go beyond the mere recitation of words to ponder with Mary the goods news of Jesus, we will begin to expose our hearts to what love is really about.

On the ceiling of the Rosary Basilica in Lourdes there is a mosaic of Our Lady with the words written underneath in French *'Par Marie a Jesus'*. Through Mary to Jesus. 'Through Mary the Word became flesh and dwelt amongst us.' Through Mary the rosary can be, as it was for Bernadette, a school where the love of Jesus takes flesh in our lives, a love to enliven and enlighten all the daily events that form the fabric of our existence.

To ponder the mysteries of the rosary. To enrol in the school of Mary. To find there a new understanding of who Jesus is and what he means to us. This is to share the prayer of the poor and the humble, the prayer of the heart, a peasant's prayer.

# 'GO TELL THE PRIESTS TO BUILD A CHURCH'

*'If you see a priest and an angel, greet the priest first.'*

Throughout history men have always built altars and erected temples to their gods. Mosques and synagogues, churches and cathedrals abound. Places of cult and creed, prayer and pilgrimage. The need is universal. Man is a religious animal. Shrines and Holy places mark his history. Apparently Lourdes is no exception to the rule. On the site of Massabielle, chapels and Basilicas have risen with great regularity.

Was this not the response to the message given by Our Lady to Bernadette, 'Go tell the priests to build a Church'? In one sense yes. But there is more in the message of Mary than just a 'building'. When Bernadette heard these words, no doubt she could only think of a chapel in honour of God, and Our Lady did mean this. But today we can hear the message in a different and deeper way. That Church is not just a building of bricks and cement. God dwells not only in the Temple but also in our hearts. He is not confined to the walls of our Church but dwells within the community of men. That Church, more than a building in his honour, is the People of God gathered around the person of the Risen Christ. In Mary's message there is a call to build up this community, a community of people who share the life and love of God and witness to that love in the world.

And that message is first given to the priests, 'Go tell the priests…' And Bernadette did. To Fr Peyramale, parish priest of Lourdes. And she continues to give Mary's message to the priests of every age; to those who, like Peyramale, are neither the best nor the worst of men. The Gospel hides nothing of the human frailty, limits, and defects of those Jesus calls to guide his people. It is not the angels (Acts 4:13) to whom Jesus entrusts his Church, nor to supermen, nor to 'gurus', but to poor men 'seduced by God like the prophet' (Jer 20:7), sustained by the Spirit and by Mary. It is to such poor men that a wonderful vocation is given to shepherd the flock. To be shepherd and not showmen, to tend the flock and not the 'till', to act not as master but as servant, not for themselves but for others, 'in the person of Christ'. To be shepherd as the Good Shepherd, seeking out men in the 'highways and byways' of life to announce the good news of God's love and compassion, to pardon and heal, restore and give hope, to give the Bread of Life to hungry hearts and reconcile all things in Christ. This is what the priest is called to build. A vocation so great and so lived in Christ that Bernadette exclaimed 'If you see a priest and an angel, greet the priest first.'

But it is not only to the priests that the message is addressed. Mary's choice of Bernadette, a simple lay person, reminds us of the vital and important role of the laity. That together, we are the Church, and we are all responsible for it.

What does it mean to be People of God? Precisely this, that we are to be 'of God'. That our lives are to be centred on Jesus, on the message of the Gospels. That we are to live a spiritual life, led and guided by the Spirit as we contemplate the mystery of God's love that Jesus reveals. That we are to live as people of the one family, sharing our goods, our burdens and our hearts.

I know many people who come to Lourdes and, before the sick and suffering, are moved to weep. It's a good sign that we still have a heart, but before the problems and pains of life it is not enough to weep. We have to act. Jesus does not call us to be spectators before the dramas of our times, but to play our part; to be active, searching positively for each other's good and welfare. He calls us not to be a people concerned with our own private individual salvation and benefit, but a people concerned for the benefit and salvation of all. We are called to 'go and bear fruit', opposing the evil of our time and creating an ever deeper brotherhood between us.

Today the People of God continue their pilgrimage toward the heavenly city of joy and light. On this journey towards the promised land of heaven, new deserts emerge that have to be faced. The new deserts of local, national and international problems include those of the poor, the oppressed, and the religious and racially discriminated.

Underdeveloped countries with massive debts to pay find themselves in an ever worsening situation of dependence upon the richer countries. Racial discrimination remains a cancer at the heart of humanity. The poor and hungry abound. Even in Europe entire families barely manage to survive. The 'new poor' sleep on benches, on pavements, and in the underground. The Church stands at the side of the poor and humble in the name of solidarity, a new name for charity as Pope John Paul II has rightly called it.

In the *Magnificat* Mary proclaims that God 'fills the starving with good things, sends the rich away empty'. The People of God are called to reflect, in tangible ways, the image of a God whose preference is for the poor. The kingdom of heaven that Jesus proclaims is not one of self-interest but of sharing our goods with each other for our mutual well being, and to enhance the quality of life, in all areas, for the benefit of mankind.

At the same time man's greatest hunger is that of knowing and experiencing the love of a God who, in the person of Jesus, has come to dwell among us. As People of God, it is for us to give to others in the world that spiritual food they hunger for, to be that voice 'crying in the deserts' of society; the voice that speaks of the dialogue of love God undertakes with humankind.

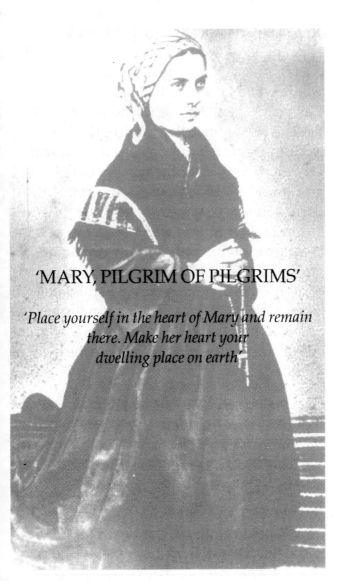

# 'MARY, PILGRIM OF PILGRIMS'

*'Place yourself in the heart of Mary and remain there. Make her heart your dwelling place on earth'*

To Bernadette, the poor girl of Lourdes, there appears not a 'Great Lady' with the airs of a queen, but a young girl, the humble young woman of Nazareth, Bethlehem, Cana and Calvary. When she names herself to Bernadette as the 'Immaculate Conception', it is not to bestow grandeur upon herself but rather to give glory to God for the wonder of his mercy and grace. When she prays the rosary with Bernadette, it is not to draw attention to herself but to ponder in her heart all the Gospel; the joyful, sorrowful and glorious mysteries of a life lived walking with Jesus through the events of his life. And so she comes to Bernadette, not as royal power, but as pilgrim of pilgrims; the one who has walked with Jesus on a pilgrimage of faith leading all mankind to the heart of a Father's love.

Here is the real Mary. The Mary of the Gospels. Mary who speaks little, who is the first to live the Gospel of poverty, the prayer of the heart, the passion of Jesus, the beginning of the pilgrim Church.

But we have lost sight of her walking the pilgrim's road before us – and with us. We have made her distant. Perhaps we think she is too 'royal' to be one of us, too 'graced' to be with us. Because Mary is Mother of God, Queen of heaven and earth, many think that perhaps she was given immunity from the pains and problems of life, immunity from the dark nights of faith common to us all. Yes, she was conceived without sin. But she was not conceived to be without pain and heartache! Yes, she is the Mother of the Risen Christ, but she is also the Mother of the Crucified One!

At the Annunciation, Mary is given a promise. A promise that she is to be mother of a child, a child to be named Jesus, Saviour of his people, Messiah, Holy One, Son of the Most High. What a tremendous moment for Mary and for the whole of humankind. What unimaginable ecstasy must have filled her heart. With such a promise the future seems assured.

And yet it is from that very moment that everything begins to go wrong, and the very promise begins to be questioned. There is 'no room in the inn' (Lk 2:7), there is no room in Judea. There is no time to feast and fuss the new born child, only time to flee with him into Egypt in fear of their lives. The promise is dealt a further blow, a prophetic warning to Mary that a 'sword will pierce her heart' (Lk 2:3), that Jesus will be opposed (Lk 2:34). And as he grows into manhood the prophecy becomes reality. He is opposed. This promised 'Son of God' is scorned, misunderstood, opposed, attacked and rejected. Indeed, everything that happens after the Annunciation seems to become a denial of the very promise made her, and humanly speaking, a complete denial as Mary stands at the foot of the cross. This Jesus, this promised Saviour, dies in a horrible agony of rejection and crucifixion. It seems the end of the promise.

Mary had no verifiable guarantee that all would be well. She was given no such assurance. Throughout the trials and difficulties she met along the road of this pilgrimage with Jesus, she must have asked herself over and over again the same question she had asked of the Angel Gabriel, 'But how will this come about?' (Lk 1:34). What sustains Mary in the dark night of not knowing the real outcome is not some special gift of foreseeing the future, but a total faith and confidence in God, an absolute surrender to his word. What God promises, he will do. 'Blessed is she who believed that the promises made her by the Lord would be fulfilled.' How will this come about? How will things work out? That question comes our way often, especially in those moments of trial and difficulty that come to all of us. But we can speak about it with Mary, share it with her heart; she will understand. For she passed on the Way of the Cross before us and she is there on the road with us. Here is the pilgrim of pilgrims, our hope and our refuge, our courage and confidence, the one who points the way. The way to faith and to trust, to confidence in the promises of God. She points the way to Jesus, that he is the 'name above all other names by which we will be saved' (Acts 4:12). She points to him as she did at Cana reminding us to 'do whatever he tells you' (Lk 2:6), for his word is of life, of love.

Before the advent of radar, sailors looked to the stars for guidance. There they would find a course to safety, hope from the raging storm. 'When the wind blows, look to the Star called Mary.' It is St Bernard who reminds us that the greatest and the brightest star of humanity is Mary, Star of the Sea; the one who is there when we are blown off course and lost in the storms of life to guide us back to the safe arms of Jesus. This is her only concern. To be a pilgrim of pilgrims, walking with us on the road, leading us to the glorious mystery of God's love.

To Bernadette Mary came, not with the aloof distance of royalty, but in the intimacy of a humble loving heart, looking at her 'as one person looks at another'. And she looks upon us with this same humble warmth, as a companion on the same road towards God, as a pilgrim of pilgrims.

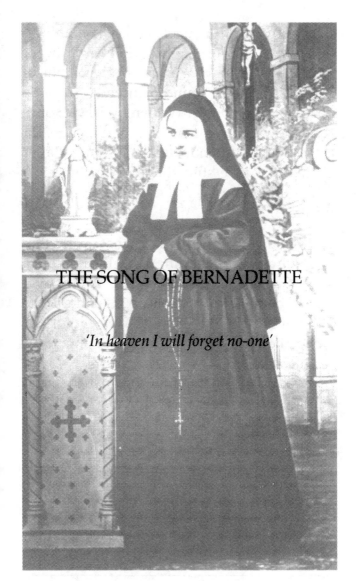

# THE SONG OF BERNADETTE

*'In heaven I will forget no-one'*

'The Lord is my shepherd, there is nothing I shall want.' A song of David, shepherd King of Israel. Written not in times of plenty but in days of famine. Famine of friends, security, peace and prosperity. Written by David; once King, now fugitive; man on the run; target for assassination. Abandoned by all, sought after by many. Worse still, sought even by a son intent on taking his father's life, his father's throne.

But the singer knows his song, that the rhythm is good and the wording is right. It takes a shepherd to know a Shepherd. And David knows his. One who is 'true to his name', who will never abandon his flock. Who 'guides us along the right path' to bring new life 'near restful waters'. Here is a Song to Jesus, Good Lord and Good Shepherd. A hymn of trust and confidence, of courage and hope. This is the Song of David the Shepherd King.

It is also the song of the little shepherdess, the song of Bernadette. Poor in the material but rich in the essential. Hungry for food but filled with love. Sick in body but well in spirit. Tried and troubled by everyone and everything but found wanting in nothing. Bernadette too knows the Shepherd's heart. The heart of the Lord in whom nothing 'shall want'.

Here is a Song for the Pilgrim,
who journeys the road to Lourdes.
For the weary and worn,
troubled and tried,
the sick and the sinner,
the one more dead than alive.
Here is a Song for the Pilgrim,
who limps along the road towards God.

'Go drink at the spring and wash yourself there.' Mary points the way to the 'restful waters' he promised; those of his love and his care. Waters of healing, waters of hope. Waters for aching hearts, worn limbs, despairing spirits.

Remember the words of the Song – let them be pondered in your heart:

The Lord is my shepherd,
there is nothing I shall want;
In green pastures he lets me lie.

Near restful waters he leads me
to revive my spirit.
He guides me in the right path
true to his name.

Even though I walk in a valley dark as death
I should feel no danger, for you are with me;
Your rod and your staff bring me comfort.

You prepare a table for me
in the eyes of my foes;
You anoint my head with oil,
and my cup overflows.

Surely goodness and mercy shall be with me
all the days of my life;
I shall dwell in the house of the Lord forever.

This is the Song of David, shepherd King of
Israel. This is the song of the little shepherdess.
The Song of Bernadette!